Funnier Bone Jokes

Ho-Ho-Ho Christmas JOKES to Tickle Your FUNNY BONE

Amelia LaRoche

Enslow Elementary
an imprint of
Enslow Publishers, Inc.
40 Industrial Road
Box 398
Berkeley Heights, NJ 07922
USA
http://www.enslow.com

Enslow Elementary, an imprint of Enslow Publishers, Inc.

Enslow Elementary® is a registered trademark of Enslow Publishers, Inc.

Library of Congress Cataloging-in-Publication Data

LaRoche, Amelia.
Ho-ho-ho Christmas jokes to tickle your funny bone / Amelia LaRoche.
p. cm. — (Funnier bone jokes)
Includes index.
Summary: "Read jokes, limericks, tongue twisters, and knock-knock jokes about Christmas. Also find out fun facts about the holiday"—Provided by publisher.
ISBN 978-0-7660-4123-3
1. Christmas—Juvenile humor. I. Title.
PN6231.C36L37 2013
818'.602—dc23

2012007712

Future editions:
Paperback ISBN: 978-1-4644-0181-7 EPUB ISBN: 978-1-4645-1094-6
Single-User PDF ISBN: 978-1-4646-1094-3 Multi-User PDF ISBN: 978-0-7660-5723-4

Printed in the United States of America

082012 Lake Book Manufacturing, Inc., Melrose Park, IL

10 9 8 7 6 5 4 3 2 1

Illustration Credits: Clipart.com, pp. 4, 7, 13, 15 (bottom), 17 (top), 18 (middle), 20, 21 (top), 23 (bottom), 28 (bottom), 29 (top, bottom), 32 (bottom), 33 (bottom), 35, 41 (top), 43 (top); Photos.com: Alexey Bannykh, pp. 25 (middle), 26 (top), Anton Brand, p. 22 (top), Brendon De Suza, p. 36 (top), Christos Georghiou, p. 44 (bottom), Dynamic Graphics, pp. 6 (bottom), 8 (left), 10, 18 (top), 28 (top), Hanna Ramanouskaya, p. 24 (top), Holger Bogen, p. 32 (top), Igor Zakowski, p. 9 (top), James Lee, p. 38 (bottom), Josef Prchal, p. 23 (top), Macy Wong, p 15 (top), mervana zaimimervana zaimi, p. 18 (bottom), Ninevian, p. 29 (middle), Oleg Iatsun, p. 39 (top), Olena Goryushko, p. 42 (cookies), Olga Koroleva, p. 14 (bottom); Shutterstock.com, pp. 1, 3, 5, 6 (top), 8 (right), 9 (bottom), 11, 12, 14 (top), 16, 17 (bottom), 19, 21 (bottom), 22 (bottom), 24 (bottom), 25 (top, bottom), 26 (bottom), 27, 30, 31 (top), 33 (top, middle), 34, 36 (middle, bottom), 37, 38 (top), 39 (bottom), 40, 42 (kids), 43, 44.

Cover Illustration: Shutterstock.com

Contents

1 The Big Guy in the Sky . . . Santa Claus!

What's red and white and red and white and red and white?

Santa rolling down a hill.

What's Santa's favorite garden tool?

The hoe, hoe, hoe.

Santa's sleigh slid sloppily.

Why does Santa use the chimney?

It soots him.

How much did Santa pay for his sleigh?

Nothing. It was on the house.

DID YOU KNOW?

Did you know that Santa Claus is based on a real person? It's true. Nicholas was a bishop in Turkey more than sixteen hundred years ago. His rich parents died when he was young, and he used their money to send secret gifts to poor people. One story says he tossed gold down a chimney so that the family's daughters could get married. The gold fell into a stocking they had hung there to dry. Today, Nicholas is the patron saint of children (and sailors, New York City, and many others).

Knock, knock!

Who's there?

Santa.

Santa who?

Santa *Claus!* You didn't know Santa's last name?

Who says, "Oh, oh, oh!"?

Santa walking backward.

What do you call someone who's afraid of Santa?

A Claus-trophobic.

Saint Nick knocked down ninety nifty knickknacks.

DID YOU KNOW?

Did you know that in Hawaii, Santa is called Kanakaloka? In England, he's Father Christmas, and in France he's Père Nöel. In Russia, he's Ded Moroz, which means "Grandfather Frost." In Wales, he's Sion Corn, or "Chimney John." In Poland, he's Gwiazdor ("Star Man") and in Sweden, he's Jultomten ("Christmas Brownie"). In Japan, he's sometimes called Santa No Ojisan, which means "Uncle Santa." You may also know him as Kris Kringle.

What do you get if Santa goes down a chimney when a fire is lit?

Crisp Kringle.

Knock, knock!

Who's there?

Interrupting Santa.

Interrupting San—

Ho, ho, ho!

Limerick

Outside in the snow, just after dawn,
Presents and gift wrap lay strewn here and yon.
The drainpipe dangled,
The lights were all tangled—
Santa had crashed his sleigh on the lawn!

Why is Santa so good at karate?

Because he has a black belt!

How can you tell when Santa is inside your house?

You can sense his presents.

Limerick

Santa's mood is generally cheery,
But one day he felt rather dreary.
Mrs. Claus asked him why,
And he said with a cry,
"Who'll deliver the gifts meant for me?"

WHAT IS A LIMERICK?

A limerick is a funny five-line poem. The first, second, and fifth lines rhyme, and the third and fourth lines rhyme. That means it has an A, A, B, B, A rhyme scheme. The third and fourth lines are also shorter than the other three. When you read limericks out loud, you can hear their beat.

2 Santa's Sidekicks: Elves and Flying Reindeer

What did the elf say when Santa took attendance?

"Present!"

What's green and white and red all over?

An elf with sunburn.

Knock knock.

Who's there?

An elf.

An elf who?

An elf who can't reach the doorbell.

FUN FACT

Clever toy inventor Charles Pajeau hired several little people, dressed them in elf costumes, and asked them to play with his Tinkertoy™ construction sets in a window at a Chicago department store during the 1914 holiday season. His publicity stunt worked! A year later, more than a million Tinkertoy™ sets had been sold. Today, the most popular toys include video games and Barbie dolls.

What does Santa use to clean his sleigh?

Comet.

Why was Santa's helper sad?

He had low elf-esteem.

Which of Santa's reindeer has bad manners?

Rude-olph.

How much rain would a rain cloud rain if a raincloud rained reindeer?

Knock, knock!

Who's there?

Santa.

Santa who?

Santa list of toys I want for Christmas. Do you think he got it yet?

What did the reindeer say to the elf?

Nothing. Reindeer can't talk.

Elves under eaves have raveled sleeves.

Which of Santa's reindeer tried out for *So You Think You Can Dance*?

Blitzen. Bet you thought I was going to say Dancer!

Limerick

The reindeer that pull Santa's sleigh
Got together to gripe one day.
Said Vixen, "It's tough
With all of that stuff!
Just how much does Santa's sleigh weigh?"

What do you call an elf with a lot of secrets?

Stelfy.

What's invisible and smells like candy canes?

Elf breath.

Limerick

An elf named Scotty grew suddenly bold.
He knew right off Santa had to be told.
"From the North Pole I'll fly!"
Santa asked, "Oh? But why?"
"It's simple," said Scotty. "I'm cold!"

FUN FACT

Did you know that reindeer are real? It's true. They're a type of deer from the Arctic, and they're called caribou in North America. Both males and females grow antlers. By the way, can you name Santa's reindeer by heart? They're—*Hey! Cover the answer and at least try to name them before you read this!* Dasher, Dancer, Prancer, Vixen, Comet, Cupid, Donner, Blitzen, and, of course, Rudolph the Red-Nosed Reindeer.

3 Carols, Cards, and Candy

What is Tarzan's favorite Christmas carol?

"Jungle Bells."

Which Christmas carol do parents like best?

"Silent Night."

What do you call a girl who starts singing when you open your door?

Carol.

DID YOU KNOW?

Did you know that by the time you've sung every verse in the Christmas carol "The Twelve Days of Christmas," you'll have named 364 gifts? It's true! That's one for every day of the year except Christmas! Here's another fun carol fact: Bing Crosby's version of "White Christmas" is the bestselling single of all time. By 2009—almost 70 years after its first release—it had sold over 100 million copies around the world, according to *The Guinness Book of Records*.

What do fish sing at Christmas?

Corals.

What carol did the man who got hit in the head start to sing?

"I Heard the Bells on Christmas Eve."

Carol Merrill Christmas-caroled merrily.

Limerick

We're told that the sweet candy cane
Is shaped by the pasture's refrain.
It's a hook made to look
Like a poor shepherd's crook;
But it's better to eat than explain.

DID YOU KNOW?

Did you know that the first printed Christmas cards were sent by a man too lazy to send handwritten ones? It's true! Sir Henry Cole of England asked a printer to whip up a batch of a thousand in 1843. Of those, only a dozen or so have survived. Billions and billions of printed cards have been sent around the world since then. In the United States, the White House alone sends as many as a million holiday cards a year.

Kris Kringle crafted creative Christmas cards.

What carol did they play at the peanut butter factory?

"Nuttin' for Christmas."

What carol did the woman who got lost in the mall sing?

"I Hope I'll Be Home for Christmas."

Limerick

When it comes to the Christmas card,
I admit I'm just not a bard.
I have a hard time
Coming up with a rhyme.
In fact, I can't think of one now. (Sorry!)

Knock, knock!

Who's there?

Norma Lee.

Normal Lee who?

Norma Lee we don't go around knocking on doors, but we're here to carol.

Knock, knock!

Who's there?

Candy.

Candy who?

Can Dee come out and play?

WHAT IS A TONGUE TWISTER?

Tongue twisters are phrases that are tricky to get out of your mouth. When you come across one, try to say it five times fast!

4 Oh, Christmas Tree! Oh, Yule Log! Oh, Wreath! Oh, My!

Why are Christmas trees such terrible knitters?

They keep dropping their needles!

Knock, knock?

Who's there?

Yule.

Yule who?

Yule never know!

How will you get onto the Internet at Christmas?

Yule log on.

What is a Christmas tree's favorite drink?

Root beer.

DID YOU KNOW?

Did you know that some evergreen trees are edible? It's true! People use the vitamin C–rich needles to make everything from spruce butter to pine powder that can be sprinkled into cookie dough. Americans chop down more than 30 million Christmas trees every year! About 350 million more are growing on U.S. tree farms.

What did the Christmas tree say to the messy house?

"I'm here to spruce you up."

Why was the candy cane afraid to cross the road?

It didn't want to get a licking!

Why do Christmas trees smell so good?

They eat orna-mints.

Limerick

When hunting for a Christmas tree,
Your options are basically three:
You can spend at a shop,
Or buy one on a lot,
Or look in the woods, where they're free!

Knock, knock?

Who's there?

Ken.

Ken who?

Ken you help me decorate the tree?

Who'll light the yule log?

Limerick

The clever young lad made a wreath
Of mistletoe, holly, and heath.
He held it above
The head of his love
And asked for a kiss underneath!

FUN FACT

The world's biggest Christmas tree isn't a tree at all. It is made from hundreds of big spotlights laid out in the shape of a tree on a hillside in Gubbio, Italy. The "tree" is 2,100 feet tall and 1,100 feet wide. Thanks to the Internet, Pope Benedict XVI lit the tree without leaving the Vatican in 2011. He just tapped the touch screen on a wireless tablet. Other wacky "trees" have included a forty-footer made from 600,000 LEGO bricks in the middle of London's busiest train station and another forty-footer made from nearly 40,000 recycled green plastic bottles in Kaunas, Lithuania.

What happened to the sad Christmas tree?

It pined away.

What did the Christmas tree say to the ornament?

"Quit hanging around and do something!"

The tall tree tipped, then toppled.

What kind of Christmas trees do dogs and cats put up?

Fur trees.

What did the barracuda use to decorate his house?

A reef.

5 What It's Really All About: Happy Birthday, Jesus

Where does Christmas come before Thanksgiving?

In the dictionary.

Limerick

Mary and Joseph rode up to the inn.
They were turned away: no reservation.
They stayed in a stable
And still they were able
To bring to the world a babe without sin.

FUN FACT

Did you know the Salvation Army's first collection kettle was a crab pot! It was plunked down at the foot of San Francisco's Market Street in 1891 with a sign that said, "Keep the Pot Boiling." Enough money was raised to give a thousand of the city's poorest people Christmas dinner that year.

Why is the Christmas alphabet one letter short?

It has no L.

How long does a fruitcake last?

Until you eat it.

DID YOU KNOW?

Did you know that the first charity Christmas card was painted by a kid? It's true! The UNICEF card featured a painting made in 1949 by a seven-year-old girl named Jitka Samkova. She lived in Rudolfo, a small town in the former nation of Czechoslovakia. After World War II, UNICEF sent food and medicine to the town. That inspired Jitka to paint children dancing around a maypole—in her words, "joy going round and round." She painted on a sheet of glass because she had no paper. Her teacher entered the art in UNICEF's contest, and it won.

What did the gardener say to the baby at Christmastime?

Sleep in heavenly peas.

DID YOU KNOW?

Did you know that when Jesus was born more than 2,000 years ago, there were only 300 million people on Earth? It's true! Today there are 7 billion people on Earth. That's a lot of birthdays.

Wise Men whispered, "What babe is this?"

Limerick

From far away Three Wise Men came
To see the babe born without blame.
A star shined bright
All through the night
To guide them straight to Bethlehem.

What comes before Christmas Eve?

Christmas Adam!

Knock, knock.

Who's there?

Mary.

Mary who?

Mary Christmas!

FUN FACT

Nobody really knows what day Jesus was born, and the Bible doesn't tell us. So in the year 350, Pope Julius I told the world that December 25 would be the official date to celebrate Christ's birth. Several non-Christian holidays were already held around then, and the pope hoped the people celebrating them would become Christians. According to the Bible, God gave the world his son, Jesus, as a way to wipe away sin. The Christmas holiday celebrates giving.

Knock, knock..

Who's there?

Warren.

Warren who?

Warren this nativity scene should I set the manger?

Where did the Wise Men get their robes shortened?

Bethlehem.

A billion brilliant, blessed bells rang out on Christ's birthday.

6 Baaaa Humbug! Animals at Christmas

What did the ram say to his wife?

"Happy holidays to ewe!"

What did the cow say on December 25?

"Moo-ry Christmas!"

DID YOU KNOW?

Did you know that animals have a patron saint? He's Francis of Assisi. We're told he set up the first live nativity scene on Christmas Eve in 1223, and an ox and a donkey were there! Today's nativity scenes often include other animals, such as the camels ridden by the Three Wise Men. Animal rights groups say it's not wise to use live animals this way, because it's too hard on them. Statues or pictures of animals usually work just fine.

Knock, knock!

Who's there?

Christmas owl.

Christmas owl who?

You sound like a regular owl to me!

Who delivers presents to dogs on Christmas Eve?

Santa Paws.

The proud pink pig opened his pretty polka-dot presents.

What does a cat on the beach have in common with Christmas?

Sandy claws.

The Christmas kittens were cuddled carefully.

WHAT IS A RIDDLE?

A riddle is a question with a surprise answer. Sometimes the answer is a pun, which is a play on words. Some riddles are funny and they make us laugh. Others are corny and make us groan. The silliest ones make us laugh and groan at the same time!

Limerick

For Christmas I asked for two kittens.
To all of my kin I have written.
How cute they would play;
In my lap they would stay—
But instead I got these blue mittens!

Knock, knock!

Who's there?

Halibut.

Halibut who?

Halibut a kiss under the mistletoe?

Limerick

While attempting to squeeze through a garret,
Santa Claus spied a talkative parrot.
Said the parrot to Santa,
"Well, can ya or can't ya?"
Puffed Santa, "I think I'll trade cookies for carrots!"

What did the calf get in her stocking?

A cow-culator.

Did you hear about the duck that went into the bakery?

They turned him into a Christmas quacker.

What did the grumpy sheep say on Christmas morning?

"Baaaaaaaa humbug!"

Who gives presents to baby sharks on Christmas Eve?

Santa Jaws.

7 Wintery Weather—Baby, It's Cold Outside!

What do snowmen eat for breakfast?

Snowflakes.

Knock, knock!

Who's there?

Will.

Will who?

Will you let me in already? I'm freezing!

DID YOU KNOW?

Did you know that the North Pole isn't the coldest place on earth? It's true! That honor goes to the South Pole. The coldest natural temperature ever recorded was –128.6 degrees Fahrenheit at a Russian research station there. By the way, the North Pole isn't a "land" at all—it's in the Arctic Ocean amid huge shifting ice sheets.

What do you get when you cross a snowman and a vampire?

Frostbite.

What falls at the North Pole but doesn't get hurt?

Snow.

Limerick

The snowman's love was heartfelt;
In a poem his feelings he spelt.
He told her he'd read it
Whenever she saw fit.
She said, "Read it before I melt!"

What do you call a snowman in the spring?

A puddle.

Knock, knock!

Who's there?

Snow.

Snow who?

Snow use. I can't remember my name.

What's white and goes up?

A confused snowflake.

What did the snowman hang over his baby's crib?

A snowmobile.

Limerick

There once was a snow girl named Tess,
Whose house was a slippery mess.
A carrot on the floor,
Coal smeared on the door—
Poor Tess had melted from holiday stress!

Why did the snowman go to Texas?

He heard they were having a chili cook-off.

Where does a snow woman keep her money?

A snow bank.

FUN FACT

To have a White Christmas in the United States, there has to be at least one inch of snow on the ground on Christmas morning. (In Canada there have to be two.) One of the weirdest White Christmases took place in 2004 when a snowstorm on Christmas Eve blew the white stuff into Houston, Texas! For the first time in decades, kids living there heard their parents complain about how other people don't know how to drive in the snow. Now they know what kids in the northern states hear every winter.

In blew a blustering blizzard.

How do you scare a snowman?

Turn on a blow dryer!

Icy icicles make icky Popsicles.

8 Have You Been Naughty or Nice?

Knock, knock!

Who's there?

Gladys.

Gladys who?

Gladys not me who got coal in her stocking!

What do you call sad kids who don't get any presents?

I don't care what you call them as long as it's not my name!

Why do kids hang stockings?

Because if they hung pants, the presents would fall right through.

DID YOU KNOW?

Did you know that more than half of American pet owners buy gifts for their furry and feathered friends during the holiday season? It's true! According to one poll, they spend an average of $46 on each pet. That amounts to millions of dollars every year. Lots of people wrap those presents and hang up stockings for their pets, too. Some even include their pet in the family photo on their holiday card, and then sign the pet's name!

Why does Santa leave presents under the tree?

Because they won't fit on top.

What happened to Santa's sleigh when he left it in a No Parking zone?

It got mistle-towed.

What wine is most often served with Christmas dinner?

"I didn't get the toy I asked for!"

Why did Sue's grades drop after the holidays?

Everything was marked down.

Why is a broken drum the best Christmas present?

You can't beat it!

The triplets threw three fits under the tree.

Limerick

Calvin asked Santa: "Are the rumors true?
Do you punish kids for things they don't do?"
Santa shook his head.
"Heavens, no!" he said.
Calvin cried, "Good! My homework's still due."

FUN FACT

Did you know that Robert Louis Stevenson "gave" away his birthday? It's true! The author of *Treasure Island* and *A Child's Garden of Verses* wrote out a deed that gave his November 13 birthday to a friend's daughter. She disliked her own December 25 birthday because it got lost in the Christmas celebration!

Knock, knock!

Who's there?

Stan.

Stan who?

Stan still! I'm trying to take a Christmas photo!

Benny's bonny beagle bit Christmas bones for breakfast.

Limerick

Unless somebody is mocking,
I find this terribly shocking—
I was nice to my sister.
When I swung, I missed her!
So why is there coal in my stocking?

9 Christmas Around the World

What nationality is Santa Claus?

North Polish.

How do sheep in Mexico say Merry Christmas?

"Fleece Navidad!"

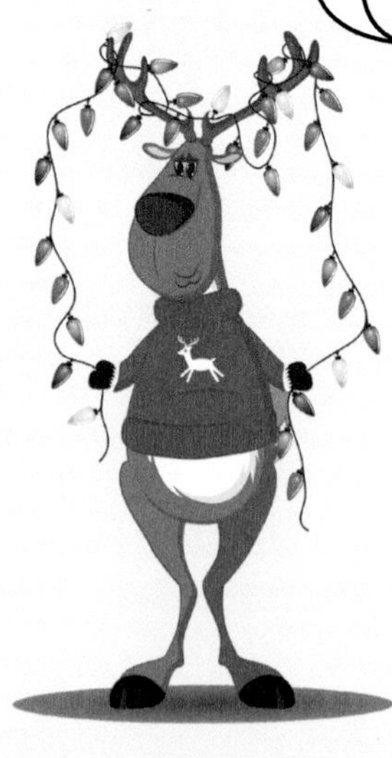

Where do people give the most sweaters at Christmas?

Chile.

DID YOU KNOW?

Did you know that people in Caracas, Venezuela, roller-skate to church in the days leading up to Christmas? It's true. As part of the fun, some kids tie a long string to their big toe and let it dangle out an open window. Skaters tug on the strings to wake up the children!

What country makes the most delicious Christmas dinner?

Turkey.

Knock, knock!

Who's there?

Irish.

Irish who?

Irish you a merry Christmas!

Rich Russians rushed to hang wreaths.

What country eats the most at Christmas dinner?

Hungary.

Which country always wants to hurry up and open all the gifts?

Russia.

Knock, knock!

Who's there?

Felix.

Felix who?

Felix Navidad!

Freezing Bolivian fleas sneeze on Christmas Eve.

Limerick

Santa flies around the whole world—
To millions of homes his sled has whirled!
So he has a strong need
To blast off at light speed
And that's why his toes are all curled.

FUN FACT

Misa del Gallo, or "Mass of the Rooster," is held on Christmas Eve in many Spanish-speaking countries. It's called this because legend says a rooster crowed on the night Jesus was born. In Germany, Heiligabend, or Christmas Eve, is said to be a time when the pure of heart can hear animals talk.

What country needs to wash a lot of dishes after Christmas dinner?

Greece.

Where did Santa go for training?

Lapland.

Limerick

In countries below the equator
The weather refuses to cater
To those wanting white
On Christmas Eve night
And that won't change sooner or later!

10 Christmas Odds and Ends

What did Mrs. Claus say to Santa on Christmas morning?

"Looks like rain, dear."

Harriet happily hollered, "Hallelujah!"

Why do reindeer have antlers?

Because it improves their reception.

DID YOU KNOW?

Did you know that candy canes were invented to keep kids quiet in church on Christmas Eve? It's true! A popular story says that in 1690, the choirmaster at a church in Germany asked a local candy maker to create the sugary sticks. He told the candy maker to add a crook to the top so it would remind kids of the shepherds who came to see the baby Jesus. Stripes didn't get added until the twentieth century.

Why did Santa leave so early last Christmas?

He had to jumpstart the reindeer.

Why is Santa so jolly?

He only works one night a year.

Knock, knock.

Who's there?

Howie.

Howie who?

Howie gonna wrap this refrigerator for Mom?

Knock, knock.

Who's there?

Candace.

Candace who?

Candace really be da last Christmas knock-knock joke in dis book?

If football players get athlete's foot, what do rocket scientists get?

Missile toe.

Limerick

Christmas cookies we will bake,
They're easy to mix and easy to make!
They taste so yummy
Inside your tummy,
But stuffing them down makes it ache.

FUN FACT

It is said that before he chose the name of Tiny Tim for his character in *A Christmas Carol,* the author toyed with three other names. Charles Dickens considered using Little Larry, Puny Pete, and Small Sam.

Many maids made merry.

Why do mummies love Christmas?

Because of all the wrapping!

Limerick

With our Christmas tree brightly glowing,
And outside it's quietly snowing,
I lie with eyes closed,
But I can't seem to doze,
Because Santa Claus is all-knowing.

Make a Silly Christmas Card

HERE'S WHAT YOU WILL NEED:

- Thick paper (if you want to get fancy, you can buy card stock designed for greeting cards—it usually comes with envelopes)
- Colored markers
- Glue stick and scissors (optional)
- Your sense of humor!

DIRECTIONS:

1. Fold the paper in half.
2. Find a holiday riddle or come up with your own.
3. Write the question on the front of your card. Draw a funny picture to illustrate it. You can draw the picture on another piece of paper and then cut it out and glue it onto the front of your card, or draw right on the card.
4. On the inside of your card, write the riddle's answer. Add some good wishes, like, "Happy Holidays!" or "Merry Christmas!" Don't forget to sign your name.

Words to Know

alliteration—The repetition of a sound in a group of words.

bard—A poet.

bishop—A church leader who ranks above a priest.

garret—A simple room at the top of a house, right under the roof.

joke—Something that is said to make people laugh.

limerick—A funny five-line poem in which the first, second, and fifth lines rhyme, and the shorter third and fourth lines rhyme.

manger—An open box that holds food or hay for farm animals.

mass—A time of worship held in Catholic churches.

nativity scene—A display showing Jesus just after he was born, surrounded by his mother, Mary; his father, Joseph; angels; and the animals that were in the stable at the time of his birth. Sometimes the shepherds, the Three Wise Men, and their camels are also shown.

pope—The leader of the Catholic church.

pun—A play on words.

riddle—A question with a surprise answer.

tongue twister—A series of fun words that can be hard to say out loud.

Vatican—The place in Rome where the pope lives and works.

vitamin—A substance found in food that is needed for good health.

Read More

Books

Dahl, Michael, Kathi Wagner, Aubrey Wagner, and Aileen Weintraub. *The Everything Kids' Giant Book of Jokes, Riddles & Brain Teasers.* Avon, MA: F + W Media, 2010.

Leno, Jay. *How to Be the Funniest Kid in the Whole World (or Just in Your Class).* New York: Aladdin Paperbacks, Simon & Schuster Children's Publishing, 2007.

Phillips, Bob. *Super Incredible Knock-Knock Jokes for Kids.* Eugene, OR: Harvest House Publishers, 2007.

Internet Addresses

Christmas Jokes for Kids
<http://www.christmasjokesforkids.com/>

Christmas Jokes, Riddles, Quotes, and Other Stuff
<http://www.brownielocks.com/ChristmasJokes.html>

Email Santa
<http://emailsanta.com/email_santa.asp>

Index

Who delivers presents to dogs on Christmas Eve?

Santa Paws.

Ready for an abundance of holiday hilarity? Trade jokes with friends about all your favorite Christmas things—Santa, reindeer, presents and more!

Ho-Ho-Ho Christmas Jokes to Tickle Your Funny Bone

About the Author

Children's book writer Amelia LaRoche loves to make people laugh. She lives in New England with a parrot named Penny Alt, who also loves making people laugh.

Other titles in the series

Funnier Bone Jokes

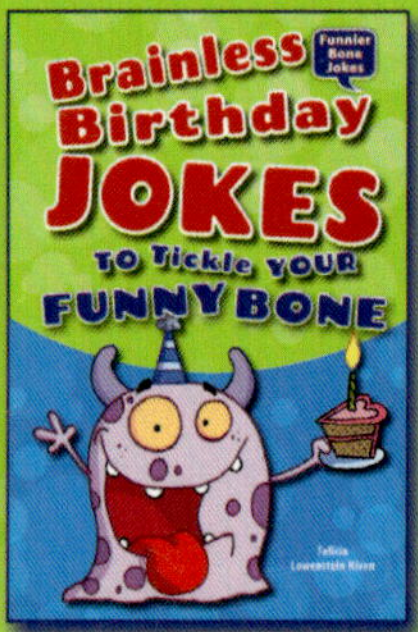

Paperback Ed. ISBN 978-1-4644-0179-4

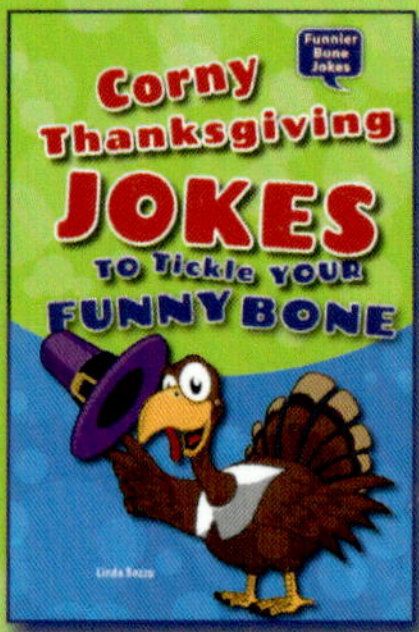

Paperback Ed. ISBN 978-1-4644-0178-7

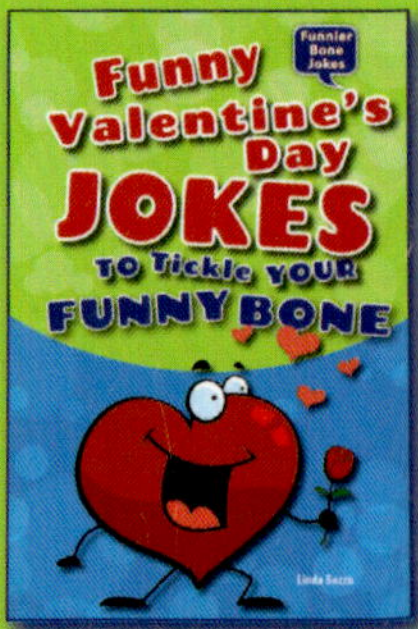

Paperback Ed. ISBN 978-1-4644-0177-0

Come to ***enslow.com*** *for more information!*

Enslow Publishers, Inc.
40 Industrial Road
Box 398
Berkeley Heights, NJ 07922
USA
http://www.enslow.com

Paperback Edition
Includes Internet Addresses

Printed in the USA

ISBN 978-1-4644-0181-7

90000

9 781464 401817

PAPERBACK EDITION

Contains at Least 10% Recycled Material